Copyright © 2023 by Ravina M Chandra

All rights reserved.

No part of this publication may be reproduced in any form, or by any means, electronic or mechanical, including photocopying, recording, or any information browsing, storage, or retrieval system, without prior permission in writing from the publisher.

Under no circumstance will any blame or legal responsibility be held against the publisher, or author, for any damages, reparation, or monetary loss due to the information contained within this book. Either directly or indirectly. You are responsible for your own choices, actions, and results.

Please note the information contained within this document is for educational and entertainment purposes only. All effort has been executed to present accurate, up to date, and reliable, complete information. No warranties of any kind are declared or implied. Readers acknowledge that the author is not engaging in the rendering of legal, financial, medical or professional advice. The content within this book has been derived from various sources. Please consult a licensed professional before attempting any techniques outlined in this book.

Published by RMC Publishers

ISBN 978-1-7386846-1-8

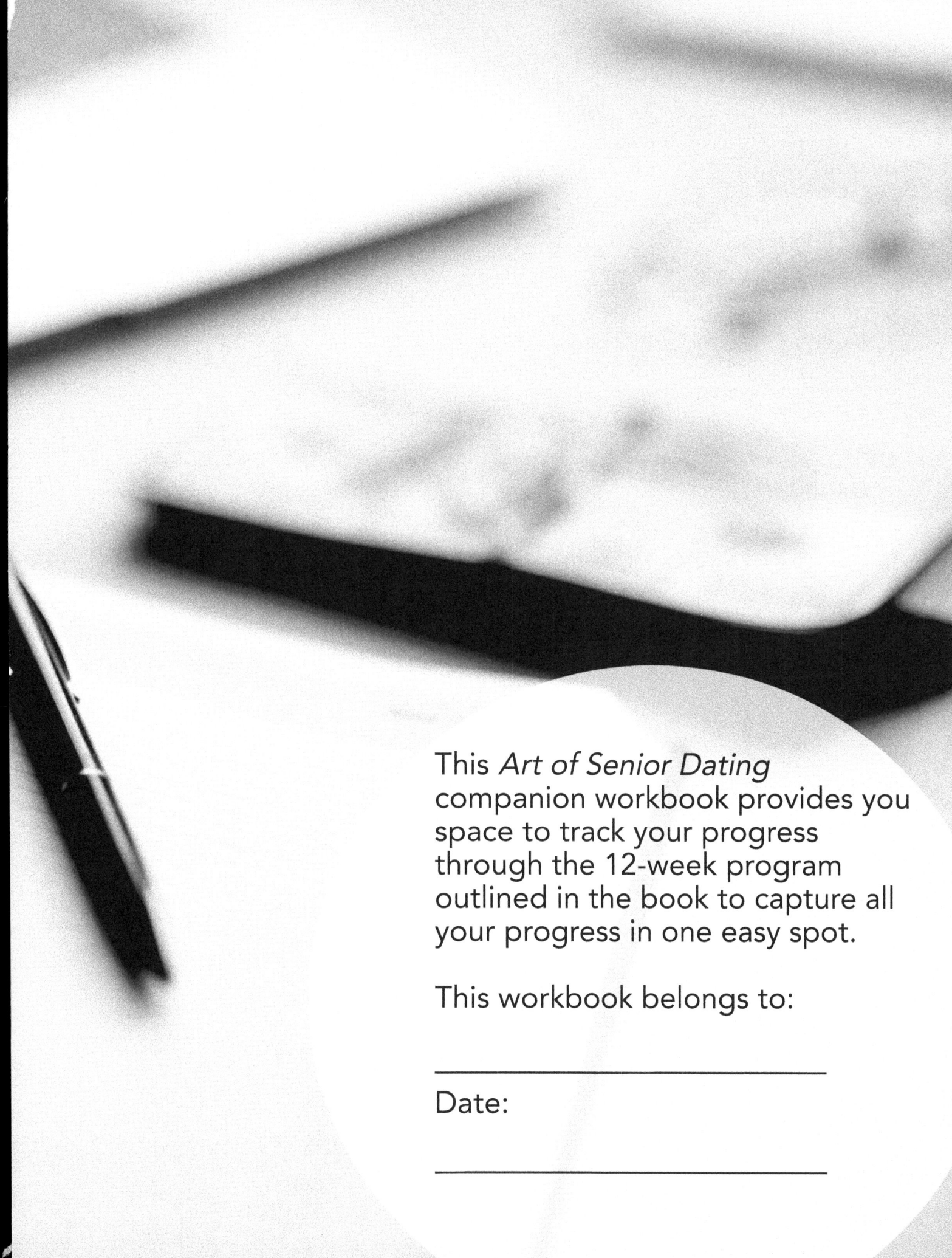

This *Art of Senior Dating* companion workbook provides you space to track your progress through the 12-week program outlined in the book to capture all your progress in one easy spot.

This workbook belongs to:

_____

Date:

_____

Week 1 - Who are You?	Week 7 - Date Smartly
Week 2 - Letting Go	Week 8 - Looking Offline
Week 3 - Upgraded You	Week 9 - Looking Online
Week 4 - Mindset	Week 10 - Don't get Obsessed
Week 5 - Who are They?	Week 11 - Learn from Mistakes
Week 6 - Get Social	Week 12 - Form Connections

Welcome

For all individuals wanting to live Vibrantly.
May your lives be fulfilling, balanced, and sparkly.

Where do you start? What do you say? No matter how confused or intimidated you might feel now, this is the first step to getting out there and meeting that special someone. Whether it's a romantic partner, travel companion, or just a new trusted friend.

Over the next 12 weeks, you are going to get inspired, build up your confidence, dig deep and discover what you really want, and make this whole dating thing fun again.

Remember to follow along at your own pace. Everyone will have their own missteps and setbacks, but as long as you keep going, you will transform yourself and your life.

Every week in this workbook has activities, actions, and checklists of things to do to keep you moving forward and progressing.

There may be setbacks, but there will also be victories. Use this tool however you need to best ensure your success. Remember to learn from your mistakes, celebrate your wins, and that this whole process is supposed to be enjoyable!

WEEK 1 Who Are You?

Having shared values is so important in any relationship, whether it's romantic or not. Understanding your own values and priorities in life can help you identify potential partners who share similar beliefs, ideas, and lifestyles. This can help minimize conflicts and lead to a stronger, more harmonious relationship, which is what most of us desire. When evaluating your values, consider aspects of your life such as your finances, personal ethics, faith, what you do for fun, and so on. Ask yourself questions to gain a deeper understanding of your values. By being honest with yourself, you can better determine what you want to stand up for in a relationship and make informed decisions in your search for a partner.

This self-reflection exercise will help you create strong relationships with people who share similar values to you, avoiding conflicts that potentially could arise in the future.

- Are finances important to you, and do you thrive on managing your money?
- What is the cleanliness level of your home, and how important is this to you?
- What is your go-to, smaller intimate gatherings or larger, more lively interactions?
- How important are environmental issues to you, and do you seek volunteer opportunities?
- When you have a surplus of funds, what do you like to spend your money on?
- Are you a spur-of-the-moment type of person, or head down, let's get planning before you implement your schedule?
- Think about your personal ethics and what is a deal-breaker for you?
- Are you free-spirited, or do you prefer taking life more seriously?
- Is silence something you need and want often, or do you require constant stimulus?
- How important is your faith to your life?

WEEK 1 ASSIGNMENT

· Capture a few photos of yourself, including one close-up of your face and also a full-body shot wearing a comfortable outfit. These pictures are for you, so don't let feeling awkward in front of the camera hold you back, simply take the photos so you can compare your appearance at the start and end of the 12-week program.

· Keep track of your progress by ticking a box every time you add a new photo to your collection.

· Take some time to reflect on your personal qualities and characteristics. The core values exercise is a good starting point, but don't limit it to this. Try to focus on words that accurately describe you in a neutral or positive light, such as joyful, busy, sincere, diligent, good listener, unbiased, quiet, etc. Write down these words in the designated space below.

Note this list will not be exhaustive. As you progress through each week of the program, you can continue to build and refine it.

WEEK 1 NOTES

This area for notes is simply to record the beginning of your journey. Take a moment to jot down your aspirations, any concerns or reservations you may have, or any key phrases that encapsulate your current thinking or emotional state. Don't overthink this, just be honest. I know it might feel challenging at first, but it will be invaluable when you look back at this section to see how far you've come. At the end of each week, you'll have the opportunity to document your progress and note how you're feeling. Think of this as the starting point for your journey ahead.

_____

_____

_____

_____

_____

_____

_____

_____

_____

_____

WEEK 1 NOTES

WEEK 2 Letting Go

Each relationship we experience leaves an impact on us, whether it be a cherished memory or a valuable lesson learned. When it comes to matters of romance or companionship, these particular relationships can be tough to let go of because of the emotional component. It's essential to give yourself permission to move forward before you can truly do so.

Only you will know when you're ready to open yourself up again.

Consider if you want to repeat the same type of relationship you had in the past or if you're truly ready for something different. Some individuals may desire the perceived security of marriage, while others prefer a more independent lifestyle with occasional or regular visits from their partner.

There is no right or wrong way to live your life, so it's crucial to be truthful with yourself about what you need at this point in time. This may include a spouse, common-law partner, companion, lover, travel companion, or friend for social outings.

It's impossible to enter a healthy relationship until you've let go of past ones. Physically say goodbye so that you can move forward in a positive way. If you don't have anyone to say goodbye to, modify this exercise to say goodbye to your previous self. Thank them for bringing you to this moment and for allowing your present and future self to evolve.

WEEK 2 ASSIGNMENT

· Keep going on your list of positive attributes. Reflect on your characteristics and embrace your honest truths. Identify words that align with the qualities and traits you aspire to have in a relationship, whether it be trustworthy or kind, for example.

Stay true to yourself in this self-reflection.

· Next, for this week, you will write a personal letter about a past relationship and express gratitude for the experience and growth it brought you.

Whether your partner is still present or has passed, take this moment to acknowledge the end of that chapter and express your hope for a bright future. This letter is for your eyes only, so feel free to write or speak your thoughts openly and honestly. Do not be tempted to send it or post it in any way. This is for you.

If you are unable to write the words down, then speak them out loud, tears and all. Celebrate your progress with a mental high-five or thumbs up once you've completed this exercise.

WEEK 2 NOTES

Use this space to write about your experiences and emotions related to a past relationship or document your progress and challenges in the journey of finding new relationships. You can also use this space to document your progress in these first few weeks and what you may be struggling with.

_____

_____

_____

_____

_____

_____

_____

_____

_____

_____

_____

_____

_____

_____

WEEK 2 NOTES

WEEK 3 Upgraded You

Part 1 - Declutter

Saying goodbye to a past relationship was a huge step, and now it's time to do the same with some of the possessions surrounding you.

This exercise encourages you to declutter your physical space in order to make room for new experiences and relationships. By letting go of old or unflattering clothes and other items in your space, you can focus on what you need and want, improving your mindset for your future search for love or companionship.

Spring cleaning can be refreshing for many of us, clearing both our minds and space. We are all different, so go at the pace that is comfortable for you.

This exercise recommends you start by decluttering one room or closet, separating everything into five piles: toss, mend, sell, share, and store. The final pile should only include sentimental items that have special meaning to you.

By clearing out the old and making space for the new, you will feel refreshed and ready to move forward.

Week 3 Upgraded You

Part 2 - Move those Muscles

This week's assignment also includes improving your physical health and well-being by engaging in physical activity that can help improve your balance and posture. It doesn't need to be a heavy-duty exercise plan; the secret is finding something doable that you can optimally carry out on a daily basis. You will be surprised at your progress just from implementing something regularly.

For those who have not been very active in some time, how about starting with a short 10-minute walk outside, if you can, taking in the scenery? Nature is known to boost your mood, so if you have any greenery near you, this is an added bonus.

If you prefer a more disciplined schedule, what about signing up for a local yoga, Pilates, or tai chi class where you might potentially meet new friends?

You should aim to do some form of movement, such as walking, yoga, stretching, or strength training, for 20 to 30 minutes each day and start slowly to build your strength and flexibility gradually. It's important to schedule your physical activity if needed to make it a consistent part of your routine.

We are all at a different starting point, so you be the judge on where to start comfortably and then move forward from there.

WEEK 3 ASSIGNMENT

· Set aside time to declutter one room this week and stick to your plan. To help with procrastination, figure out which day and time in the week you will do this task. Once you get going, the momentum should kick in, and you will be amazed at how good you feel.

Each time you clear a space in your home, check off a box.

☐ ☐ ☐ ☐ ☐ ☐

· Choose a form of movement, such as walking, yoga, stretching, or strength training, to perform for about 20-30 minutes daily. Start slow and gradually increase your effort. If you need to start with just 10 minutes a day, that's perfectly fine too.

Form of Movement	Duration

WEEK 3 ASSIGNMENT

· Continue adding positive words to describe yourself. Reflect on your progress and celebrate your accomplishments, big or small. Acknowledge the steps you have taken towards a happier and healthier life.

· Take note of any new insights or lessons you have learned. Are there any changes you have noticed in your physical, mental, or spiritual state? Writing down your experiences will help you reflect and solidify your progress and can also serve as a source of inspiration for you and others you share your journey with.

_____

_____

_____

_____

_____

WEEK 3 NOTES

WEEK 3 NOTES

WEEK 4 Mindset

As we change the physical world around us, our outlook begins to evolve as well. If you focus on the good things you do, you will be reminded that you are a good person. Maybe you've done favors for people, complemented others, or made donations to a charity or noble cause.

· Keep track of the positive things you do each day and reflect on them regularly. This will help reinforce your belief in yourself and increase your feelings of gratitude.

· Read books and articles that uplift and stimulate your mind, and consider exchanging books with friends to socialize and expand your knowledge. Lifelong learners are generally curious, and this makes it easier for them to carry out conversations with others.

· Practicing gratitude regularly actually rewires your brain and helps you deal with stress and toxic emotions more effectively like negativity.

· Don't forget to continue with the previous three weeks' assignments, including finding new positive ways to describe yourself, decluttering a room or drawer each week, and maintaining your chosen movement activity. Continuously work on bettering yourself, both physically and mentally and reap the rewards that are on their way.

WEEK 4 ASSIGNMENT

- Continue with your self-improvement journey by carrying on with the tasks from Weeks 1 to 3.

Positive Attributes

Spaces Decluttered

☐ ☐ ☐ ☐ ☐ ☐

Physical Activity

Form of Movement	Duration

WEEK 4 ASSIGNMENT

- Document the acts of kindness you show to others and the books you are reading. Referencing this list, along with your previous lists, likely will make you feel like a newer, brighter version of yourself.

Kind Deeds	Books

- Select one or two motivational quotes and one or two empowering affirmations to display in your bathroom, office, or kitchen as a constant reminder of what's important in your life.

Quotes or Affirmations

WEEK 4 NOTES

WEEK 5 Who are They?

Once you've got a healthy handle on who you are and what you want in a relationship, you can extend your gaze out into the world to see who might match your core values and the type of partnership that works for you.

To find a fulfilling relationship, it's important to first understand your own values and what you're looking for in a partner. Look for someone who compliments your life in areas where you might feel a gap. Later-life relationships are no longer limited to a marriage, so don't feel pressured to fit into society's mold. Start by viewing yourself differently and creating the life you desire rather than settling or doing what is expected of you.

While it's great to have a specific ideal situation or person in mind, it's also important to be flexible and distinguish between what is essential and what is merely nice to have in a relationship. Don't be discouraged if you don't find someone who meets every single one of your criteria, focus on what truly matters.

For this week's assignment, continue with the tasks from the previous four weeks. Create a comprehensive list of your wants, needs, and deal-breakers without limiting yourself. Expect new thoughts to arise as you progress. Stay open-minded throughout the process.

Remember, nothing is set in stone, and at any time, you can tweak these lists and move traits around.

WEEK 5 ASSIGNMENT

Positive Attributes

Spaces Decluttered

☐ ☐ ☐ ☐ ☐ ☐

Physical Activity

Form of Movement	Duration

Kind Deeds, Books, and Quotes

Kind Deeds	Books or Quotes

WEEK 5 ASSIGNMENT

- Draft your list of wants, needs, and deal-breakers without finalizing it. More ideas will pop into your mind as we work through the next few weeks.

Remember to keep an open mind at all times.

Wants	Needs	Deal-Breakers

WEEK 5 NOTES

WEEK 6 Get Social

Once you decide to get out and meet new people, you may need a refresher on how to flirt or even start a conversation with someone new. After a period of being on your own or not dating for some time, getting back into socializing can feel a bit scary. But don't let self-doubt hold you back. Think of it as re-learning a familiar skill, like riding a bike. With practice, you will become more confident and competent in these areas.

To kickstart your socializing, start with very simple conversations. As you keep practicing, talking to people will become easier. Here are a few helpful tips:

- Ask questions that require more than just a "yes" or "no" answer
- Try to stay relaxed, and don't fidget, as the other person may sense if you are tense
- Allow pauses in the conversation without feeling the need to fill in every bit of silence
- Smile and be open to listening to the other person
- Try not to be distracted and stay focused on the person in front of you
- Maintain a positive attitude

By taking small steps and engaging in conversations, your self-esteem will grow, and you will become more connected to the world around you. Try not to hold back; you have so much to offer.

WEEK 6 ASSIGNMENT

Positive Attributes

Spaces Decluttered

☐ ☐ ☐ ☐ ☐ ☐

Physical Activity

Form of Movement	Duration

Kind Deeds, Books, and Quotes

Kind Deeds	Books or Quotes

WEEK 6 ASSIGNMENT

· Use your list of wants, needs, and deal-breakers as a guide when observing other couples, both real and fictional, to identify what aligns with your values. Remember, this list is not set in stone and may change as you grow and reflect on your future.

· Make an effort to have a conversation, small or big, with someone in your network each day, whether in person or over the phone. Keep track of each friend you reach out to.

· Schedule at least one or two social events this week, such as coffee with a friend or a family member, a walk, or a bite to eat. Plan your next event immediately after each one to maintain momentum. Start building a list of ideas, as this habit should be established throughout the duration of the program. Keep track of each event by marking it off with one of the symbols. By the end of this program, this practice should be a firmly established habit.

WEEK 6 NOTES

WEEK 7 Dating Smartly

Online dating offers the opportunity to connect with new individuals, but it's crucial to avoid common mistakes to ensure a safe experience. There are some common mistakes people make that you can easily avoid.

Here are a few common things to avoid:

- Typos or misspelled words: People form quick judgments, and a single typo can negatively impact that first impression.

- Sharing personal details: Medical information, personal details that would let them find you in real life before you are ready, or hinting at family drama are never good icebreakers.

- Being generic: Avoid generic responses, and instead share specific interests to differentiate yourself from others.

- Relying solely on one person: Don't get too attached too quickly, and instead, keep an open mind, so you don't put all of your eggs in one basket.

- Lie: Don't post outdated photos or falsely claim to enjoy activities you haven't tried. Be true to yourself and what you want.

- Sit back and wait: Don't wait for someone else to reach out, be proactive and send that first message. No mind games, no waiting around, just do it.

- Being overly critical: Remember that creating a profile can be nerve-wracking, so don't judge others harshly or quickly for not having a perfect profile.

WEEK 7 Dating Smartly

Romance Scams

Beware of online scams. Scammers create fake identities, gain trust, and then ask for money. These scams can happen to anyone, even the smartest and most cautious person. It's sad, but it's reality. So look out for these red flags to avoid being scammed online:

- They are absent for long periods of time with vague excuses
- Their English is awkward and lacks common phrases or expressions
- Their initial message is not personalized and doesn't mention anything from your profile
- They try to move the conversation off the dating platform
- They offer video chats, visits, or proof of existence, but constantly cancel
- They ask for money, gift cards, or any financial information

Trust your instincts, and don't feel obligated to continue a conversation if it makes you feel uncomfortable.

This week, keep up with your tasks from Weeks 1 to 6. Continue writing your thoughts down in your journal, keep moving, reading, practicing gratitude, and finding opportunities to spread joy to the people around you.

WEEK 7 ASSIGNMENT

Positive Attributes

Spaces Decluttered

☐ ☐ ☐ ☐ ☐ ☐

Physical Activity

Form of Movement	Duration

Kind Deeds, Books, and Quotes

Kind Deeds	Books or Quotes

WEEK 7 ASSIGNMENT

- Update your list of wants, needs, and deal-breakers.

Every day, take the opportunity to connect with someone in your circle. Track your progress by checking a box for each friend you reach out to.

☐ ☐ ☐ ☐ ☐ ☐

Plan one to two social events this week, such as meeting a friend (new or old) or a relative for coffee, a walk, or a casual meal. Continuously build momentum by planning your next outing after each event. Make a commitment to participate in at least one activity outside of your home.

I have enrolled in the following group:

_____

_____

_____

_____

WEEK 7 NOTES

WEEK 7 NOTES

WEEK 8 Looking Offline

When searching for someone, keep the concept of a "target-rich environment" in mind.

If you are looking for men, go somewhere where there are single men present. This may sound obvious, but it may also require you to step out of your comfort zone.

Spend some time brainstorming where you would expect to find people with similar interests and lifestyles as you. Here are some locations to consider:

- A coffee shop for early birds
- A library or bookstore for book lovers
- A gym for fitness enthusiasts
- Community dance for those who like to socialize
- A film festival for moviegoers
- A volunteer event for those who love helping others
- A place of worship for those with similar spiritual beliefs

Networking is key and may require some practice to improve this. You have taken steps to improve and expand your horizons and become that better version of yourself, so share your growth with the world.

WEEK 8 ASSIGNMENT

Positive Attributes

Spaces Decluttered

☐ ☐ ☐ ☐ ☐ ☐

Physical Activity

Form of Movement	Duration

Kind Deeds, Books, and Quotes

Kind Deeds	Books or Quotes

WEEK 8 ASSIGNMENT

- Keep a list of your wants, needs, and deal-breakers close at hand.

- Connect with someone in your network daily, whether it be in person or by catching up with an old friend on the phone. Keep track of each interaction by checking a box for each friend you reach out to.

☐ ☐ ☐ ☐ ☐ ☐

- Plan and attend one or two social events this week, and participate in the group or activity you joined previously. Check a box each time you engage in a social activity.

☐ ☐ ☐ ☐ ☐ ☐

- Identify at least three target-rich environments.

Target Rich Environments

- Get a current photo of yourself enjoying a hobby or activity. You can hire a professional photographer, take a selfie, or have a friend or relative assist you. Make sure the photo is taken in natural light that highlights your features and brings out that smile on your face. Keep track of new photos by checking off a box for each new photo of yourself.

☐ ☐ ☐ ☐ ☐ ☐

WEEK 8 NOTES

WEEK 9 Looking Online

By now, you should be feeling revitalized and armed with new ideas to brighten up your life. It's time to take the next step. Your home is uncluttered, and you have a clear understanding of who you are and what kind of person would fit into your future.

We'll now move online.

If you're feeling nervous, that's okay. We already addressed potential pitfalls in Week 6, so you're well-prepared for the worst. It's time to make yourself visible in the digital world.

Start with a strong introduction, crafting a narrative that will attract the right type of attention. Think of it as writing an introduction for a biography. Rather than listing facts, focus on your passions and let your energy shine through, highlighting what is unique and intriguing about you.

Be proud and confident, and don't hesitate to showcase the best photo you have of yourself.

Here are the top 5 dating sites to try:

Match - they have been around for over 20 years and usually have the largest pool of available people

eHarmony - does more narrowing down based on interests

Silver Singles - focused on your ideal age range

Senior Match - is great for finding friends for travel or activities

Our Time - draws more active people and has a relaxed feel

WEEK 9 ASSIGNMENT

Building your online presence can be daunting if you've never done this before. Don't let it hold you back from continuing your progress made in Weeks 1-8. However, if you need a break, take it and return to your routine when you feel ready.

Don't stress over creating the perfect online dating profile. Have fun with it, and choose photos that showcase your true self. You can always make adjustments later; the important thing is to start and find what platform works best for you.

Remember, learning is part of the process.

Platform	Suitability	Profile Created
eHarmony		
Match		
Silver Singles		
Senior Match		
Our Time		
Other		

WEEK 9 NOTES

WEEK 9 NOTES

WEEK 10 Don't Get Obsessed

You are now officially out there. This next point is very important. Limit your online dating activity to just one hour a day. This should be enough time to stay up to date with messages and make thoughtful decisions about how to proceed. Spending more time will start to feel like a time-waster and take you away from all the great habits you've created for your daily life.

Here are some tips to make the most of your time:

- Pay attention to tone - a person's profile and responses can give you insight into their character.

- Be open-minded - if someone keeps appearing on your feed but doesn't seem interesting, ask an open-ended question to see if there's potential.

- Stay true to your standards - don't compromise on your deal-breakers, even if you aren't getting immediate results. This takes time.

- Be authentic - pretending to be someone you're not can lead to a bad match and can convey insecurity.

- Practice - like with all skills, the more you do, the better you'll get.

- Leave a positive impression - show others that you value them, stay positive, and enjoy your interactions.

WEEK 10 ASSIGNMENT

Positive Attributes

Spaces Decluttered

☐ ☐ ☐ ☐ ☐ ☐

Physical Activity

Form of Movement	Duration

Kind Deeds, Books, and Quotes

Kind Deeds	Books or Quotes

WEEK 10 ASSIGNMENT

· Make sure to keep your list of wants, needs, and deal-breakers handy.

Connect with someone in your network daily, whether through in-person conversation or a call to an old friend to touch base.

Check off a box for every friend you reach out to.

· Plan and participate in one or two events this week, including any new clubs, groups, or activities you joined. Check off a box every time you head out for something social.

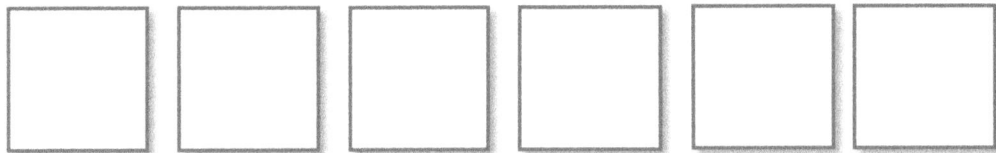

· Refine your online dating profile based on feedback from those who message you and what seems to resonate with them.

Platform	Profile updated	New Photos Added
eHarmony		
Match		
Silver Singles		
Senior Match		
Our Time		

WEEK 10 NOTES

WEEK 11 Learning As You Go

With each new person you encounter, you will find a mix of traits that match your expectations and some that don't. It's up to you to decide what you find acceptable.

Take the lessons you have learned so far and adjust your approach as needed. Even not-so-great feedback can be valuable in helping you improve and move forward. As long as you continue to learn from setbacks, difficulties, and challenges, you will continue to grow.

With just one week remaining, the activities from Weeks 1 to 10 should now feel like second nature. Your home has minimal clutter, you are reading books and finding inspirational quotes, and you have taken steps to leave your past behind and build a brighter future.

WEEK 11 ASSIGNMENT

Positive Attributes

Spaces Decluttered

☐ ☐ ☐ ☐ ☐ ☐

Physical Activity

Form of Movement	Duration

Kind Deeds, Books, and Quotes

Kind Deeds	Books or Quotes

WEEK 11 ASSIGNMENT

· Evaluate your list of wants, needs, and deal-breakers on a regular basis as you meet new people and assess how well they align with each category.

· Connect with someone in your network every day, either in person or by calling a friend to touch base. Check off a box for every friend you reach out to.

☐ ☐ ☐ ☐ ☐ ☐

· Plan and attend one or two social events this week, including participating in clubs, groups, or activities that you find enjoyable. Keep track of your social engagement with a check for each event attended.

☐ ☐ ☐ ☐ ☐ ☐

· Monitor your online dating progress daily unless you feel it's necessary to take a break to focus on deepening a connection with one particular person.

Platform	# of Messages	Keep or Abandon?
eHarmony		
Match		
Silver Singles		
Senior Match		
Our Time		

WEEK 11 NOTES

WEEK 12 Form Connections

As you progress through this journey, your life will continue to expand with new experiences, new conversations, and new relationships. You will have more opportunities to share your gifts with more people.

This can bring new challenges as you navigate integrating new people into your social and personal circles. Be mindful that while you may be excited about these changes, others around you may feel protective or unsure. Remember that this journey is yours, and you started it with a specific goal in mind.

Keep your focus on what you truly desire, and never settle for anything less than what you deserve. Do not let the effort you've put in over the past 12 weeks go to waste.

Though stepping out of your comfort zone may have been scary at first, now is a great time to reflect on your growth and compare the improvements in your life now to how you felt in Week 1.

WEEK 12 ASSIGNMENT

· Review your progress and maintain those healthy habits from the previous 11 weeks that support you and keep you on track. Incorporate social events, reading, conversations, and online experiences into your routine as part of your newfound self.

· Consider how your life has improved for the better.

· Write down how proud you are of how far you have come and how much stronger and happier you may feel now. This applies whether you're with a potential mate or single.

· Take an 'after' picture of yourself, both a headshot and a full-body shot, and compare your appearance from when you first started this 12-week plan. It's not about looking thinner; it's the radiance in your eyes and smile that truly matters.

· Congratulate yourself on how far you've come!

If you want to share any successes or ask me any questions, contact me at:

ravina@ravinachandra.com

WEEK 12 NOTES

WEEK 12 NOTES

WEEK 12 NOTES

WEEK 12 NOTES

www.ingramcontent.com/pod-product-compliance
Lightning Source LLC
Chambersburg PA
CBHW042036100526
44587CB00030B/4456